Flat Sole Studio
St. Paul, Minnesota

Flat Sole Studio
St. Paul, Minnesota
flatsolestudio.com

Copyright © 2024 John Davis

All rights reserved. No part of this publication
may be reproduced in whole or in part
without written permission of the publisher.

Library of Congress Cataloging-in-Publication Data
Library of Congress Control Number: 2024935131
 ISBN: 979-8-8692-6080-2 (Ingram pbk)
 ISBN: 979-8-320434-96-4 (Amazon pbk)

Credits
Blake Hoena, editorial direction
Flat Sole Studio, cover design and book layout

Photo Credits
Shutterstock, cover
Kayla Davis, author photo

Special thanks to Lori Davies, Sharon Hashimoto, Blake Hoena, Sue Hylen, Susan Landgraf, Colleen McElroy, Heather McHugh, Robert McNamara, Sati Mookherjee, Arlene Naganawa, Lisa Sarsfield, Tom Snyder, Michael Spence, Ann Spiers, David Wagoner, Conrad Wesselhoeft, and John Willson.

Guard the Dead

poems of war and honor
by John Davis

Acknowledgments

Poems in this collection have appeared previously in the following journals, a few under different titles: "Inspection" and "Stationed in Yorktown," *Alphabet Box*; "After Morning Muster," "Boarding the MV from Monrovia," and "Our War," *As You Were Military Review*; "What Was that Book?," *Bluestem*; "Navajo Code Talkers," *Chaffin Journal*; "Longview Parade" and "The Dead Are Still Shaving," *Cider Press Review*; "Icicles at the Edge of the Koi Pond," *Crab Creek Review*; "Wind Inside the River," *Fahmidan Journal*; "Lyon Years Later," *Flint Hills Review*; "Lifelong," *Open Road Review*; "Final Syllables," *Passager*; "Napoleon's Penis," *Pinyon*; "Before Draft Numbers" and "What we Hold," *Poetry Corners*; "Survival," *Poetry Super Highway*; "Coming Home," *Roanoke Review*; "Julius Rosenberg Murmurs from the Dead," *Rose Red Review*; "Double Reverse," *Song of Eratz Poetry Review*; "Yalta," *Tinderbox Poetry Journal*: "Eulogy for a Bullet," *Twelve Mile Review*; "For the Last Time," *The Virginia Norma*; "Bob Beamon's Leap" and "Margot Volk in the Wolf's Lair," *Zone 3*

"Returning Student" appeared in the anthology *Workers Writers: More Tales from the Classroom*.

for the memory of my parents, John & Harriet Davis

i

Longview Parade

When the dead speak to me, I ask them
    to be patient while I mark time
in the color guard, legs starched-stiff
    as my Coast Guard uniform. It's hot
as gas flares. Veterans in lounge chairs

tilt their heads, suck on beers.
    Marching ahead of us a girl in glitter silver
twirls a baton, *whoa-whoas* the crowd.
    The real delight is Michael Landon
riding behind us in a convertible.

Yes, Little Joe Cartwright. Charles Ingalls.
    As a boy Michael rescued his mother
from suicide which haunted him. He wet
    his bed. She hung his sheets in the window
for all to see his shame. Michael waves.

My left arm cramps from holding a rifle.
    Seagulls drift by from the Columbia River.
7000 miles away in a barracks latrine
    my ex-camp counselor holds a barrel
in his mouth. It is cold as the veterans' beer.

The bullet is warm as a campfire. His trigger
    finger is wet as splashes from boys on rafts.
We mark time. March on. A murder of crows
    watches from a tree. A ball rolls in front of us
like a grenade. The crowd cheers.

Sideways

It may have been 1964 in Seattle,
Vietnam heating up,
but in our house it was 1864.
Mother retold the Battle of Nashville
battle charge by battle charge
tightening her jaw and spitting *Yankee*
like a rotten prune: *Yannnkee*.
Cousin this died. Cousin that died honorably,
every man named Colonel as far as I could tell.
I should be proud to wear a uniform.
Father poured more wine and toasted
the hunters in the bird shooting prints.
With her fork, Mother snapped
my elbows on the table

the way the drill instructor snapped
at me years later.
I was such a shitbird, disgrace to my country.
Did my mother send me here to piss him off?
No wonder we weren't winning Vietnam
with a shitbird like me who had a seabag
stuffed up his ass. I didn't care

about communists in Vietnam as I elbowed
my way across the compound, sideways on all fours,
spitting out dirtballs the size of prunes,
bleeding in the heat, wondering why war
is so handsome at a dinner table.

Guard Duty Gloucester City, New Jersey

guard the night gate. no shell casings
like Feenstra guarding the gate
in the Mekong. no fatigues like Feenstra. no
eardrum-ringing hum. no bullet-static blasts.
no language to hate. just a draft number here.
the slopes and angles of 44. the night
a sponge of headlights. flick on flick off.
at worst a blaring burst of car radios. seamen
drunk returning from liberty.

in the Mekong a symphony of bugs of spit
of clicks. hiss and steam of footsteps threading
brush. what is the firepoint the flashpoint of night.
hinge of wind. flick of thumb on a safety. the moon—
polished chrome. raid of VC in the blue dark.
sweat the late May heat. no way to censor
adrenaline in the Mekong. Squad leaders missions
mortars. by morning missing arms missing legs.
blood drained.

across continents skeletons drift. scars
on their clavicles. these are the headlights
and noise the grillwork and engines gunning up
to this gatehouse saying *let us in. guard us.*
no more lullaby of bullets. sweat beads the horizon.
a silk fabric all black. we the guard dogs. laymen angels.
waiting to lay our muzzles down. sniff thin blades.
guard the dead and the undead. against our paws
the night wind blows the heat of blood.

Our War

I'm not *gook* says Watanabe.
I'm *Japanese* which was *gook*
in our fathers' war but our fathers
are pillowed and fat in front of a tube
hundreds of miles away. We're polishing brass,
cleaning M-16s. On a radio Aretha blasts
Chain Chain Chain through the barracks.

Gonna get me a gook Wilbur grins.
Wilbur's fighting his own war, likes men,
tried climbing into my bunk, wanted
to keep warm. He swaggers his ass
to the head. Charlie Company's war
is to be P-I Perfect tomorrow at Inspection,
earn liberty, find a bar and a barmaid.

Just a barmaid, smells of wild rose,
hair thin like mist. Wilbur will find
a man. Lots of men take liberties.
Watanabe and I will see pictures of the latest
Buddhist to sit cross-legged in Saigon,
burn himself into the figure
his life has become.

Amidships

We made the bunk room
into a ship, Sister and I
on rain-blitz mornings,
imagined branches slapping
the window were twenty-foot waves.
The cat curled in her rogue joy.
The overhead light sputtered
to ward off bad luck
while we balanced on the ladder
hung from the upper bunk
(the ucker bunk).
All the blue floor became
all sea, infested with sharks,
dark jaws about to chop off limbs.

Once upon a today I've built
a small ship inside myself
small mast, small rigging
small sails, small sheets.
A mock-up to pilot the seas
I've never sailed. Ever
in phantom, small hull
small keel, small bowsprit.
Below decks everything
well-stowed, braced against
typhoons and sharks.
Small rudder, small shrouds
a small captain's bunk
that the storms never find.
A balance on the sea.

River Patrol

My face surfaces in the glass
water of the river, a frail flame
running downstream, edge of dusk

between bulk carriers and container ships.
A part of me points
in four directions like a hawk,
wings crossed against the sky.

A part of me owns a small fortune—
late-light clouds twisted
into gold bands a bride acquires.
One ring size fits all.

The steady hum of the engine
tunnels under the current.
The hull washes off upstream scum.

No one drowns today. No one needs
a tow. No speedboat needs boarding.
Shadows of the Steel Bridge are dark,

thin fires, veins of the coming night.
You might say our boat is combing
the lovely hair of the Willamette.
The river has been grooming itself all day.

Wind Inside the River

We have found fog under the dry night.
It bends over us, silent as soil, a mouth

of spirits whose secrets are hidden in stone.
The water here is the wind, the stars saltless

as young salmon swimming downstream.
The celebration of eggs into silvery skin,

the howling hunger of moonlight through clouds,
the woods, the stream, the rocks below summer sky,

the robes of thunder—we hold them in amazed
laughter as if we are deer-hoofed

and dart through the forest. We do not cry
like thorns in berry vines or the dried light

stored in bark. We do not gleam like black eyes.
We do not scatter bones like flecks of daylight.

Within our sleep we set fire to our bodies,
breathe evenly, a song of quiet warmth.

Stationed in Yorktown

To run among the ghosts of soldiers
who knelt on deerskins knelt
on dirt and struck the air with flintlock
muskets begging it to open to admit them
as they were, young grunts young as I
wanting the war to be done. Here the tunnels
of air to run through. Here the smell of smoke.

Here the birth of deaths. Legs like mine
wore the body. The ballast they carried
like mine was the heavy snow of the heart.
What didn't shiver was the hum of home,
voices there, wind in night trees, smells
of jasmine, squish of toes in clover, branches
lit in late light. Who doesn't want to return
to the song they were born in. Keep running
and carry the cold. Wind through the trees
is the flute calling us home.

December Current

So cold the river, it wanted to shiver
feel its hackles fur-up like caterpillars.
It wanted to fling down its arms
kneel on embers, warm itself
with a bottle of rot-gut, feel its blood
cling again to bones, each joint unclouded
welcomed to warmth, tongue uncringed
wanted to feel nerves laugh in its face

instead of running cold, thickening the cold
that was stone-cold as the barrels of a shotgun
left in a shed. To open its hands
feel starlight drinking from its palms
a dawn inside unbending its back. To limber
in a warm run, no need to pray in secret
with chapped lips or wonder how moonlight
lengthens a shadow through the night.

At some point in your life you want
to be a jellyfish and clone yourself.

Stopping By The Old Base
in response to W.D. Ehrhart

What I came here to find
was never mine. After the years
I didn't salute, didn't stand
butt-tight during inspection,
coffee breath of the captain
wheezing into me as he checked
my neck, coat and medals,

I hear the accent of gunner's mates,
thick as tar, cleaning M-16s, the fun
of the young about to go to war,
faces bright as plastic roses.
I forget what my arms
look like with insignias and stripes,
forget what marching and squared-

corners do to you: you're in
a dictator's palace that's burning
and you're guarding his throne.
What we lost was not ours. If we
didn't lose it here, then on the 44-footer
in swells or LORAN stations
or a big white one or breaking ice.

I have come here to find
what I was before whitecaps
and swells washed through nightmares.
We are what we have lost
and when we find it, it's like finding
an arrowhead and fingering it,
wondering what we have fought for.

ii

Watering the Tomato Plant

her skirt billowed in the scrubby grass
first date the day moon a wafer
on a Saturday my mother and her date
swish-swish of feet keeping pace
with their laughter easy laughter
his syllables as smooth as phosphorus
a promise to call the next day
he didn't call the next day
December 7th he called on
December 9th wasn't allowed to call
but he called and said he was shipping out
didn't want her to think he wasn't
thinking of her

never heard never knew what the war
had done to him but she wondered
to me in her final month what
had become of Dean Wilgus
from Columbus Missouri could I
discover for my mother who was taking
fifteen drugs a day didn't walk well but well
enough to water her tomato plant twice a day
she remembered him like a mug
of warm milk the nights she couldn't sleep
swallowed down a glow
the very groove the tune
of romancing on her death bed

Double Reverse

Leaves have wrapped tired knots
around themselves against a ground
suddenly muddy and more muddy among
our thundering shoes. Men too old
to play football are two-hand touching
a Thanksgiving Day. We are thankful
for ligaments and spines and standing
water that we slide through, tuck the ball,
slide, splash, crash.
                      It's fourth down.
The air smells of wet wash. Our mud faces
hang like wrinkled jeans. In the huddle
Doug diagrams a play in his palm,
looks eye to muddy eye, exacting
as a Pilgrim might have been before walking
on the new shore and pulling a double reverse
on the Wampanoag people years before designing
the Statue of Liberty play.

Falling Man

He drops like a missile
tan coat, left leg bent
as though he is slouched
on a sofa watching
a game show. He knows
the answer as he hurtles
120 miles per hour.
Head down, North Tower
behind him in rows
of steel bars. He has no
beef with gravity or air
that billows his black pants
his black goatee, perfectly
vertical, the pose
he poses at night after
kissing his wife
after a final sip of water
and long breath. There is no
flail in his falling. Morning rises
and opens as he drops
in the high heat, an arrow,
a diagrammed sentence,
an active verb.
He knows the answer:
a final breath.

Yalta

Here comes the dark, the same dark
that night might have wound around
FDR at Yalta, his heart worn down
like a '27 Ford. He shuffled, dragged
the dark in his legs, followed the limestone
marble of the moon across the Black Sea.

Who is to say the lunar eclipse this night
is not the blood-red glow of Dresden
smoldering or Churchill's cigar or his face
burning when repeating again and again
*The Spanish ships I cannot see for they
are not in sight,* ridding himself of his lisp.

And if the wind is not the ghosts of
Soviet millions still starving in their graves,
what does the night tell us of Stalin's
withered arm, his club foot aching. I open
history books fanned on the floor, hear
syllables of the dead, their stiff tongues asking.

Margot Wolk in the Wolf's Lair

Margot might have loved risotto or the mornings
of oatmeal, the sky as virginal as golden plums.
She might have sprinkled basil as she twisted
spaghetti, tasted it while a hint of garlic

puckered her lips and she shivered the way
she once shivered after kissing her husband.
But as Hitler's reluctant food taster, she tasted
for poisons among the stewed fruits: tiny bites.

Her eyes darted left, darted right. She chewed
in a room with a guard. If Hitler died, she would die
first. And she ate baked potatoes with cottage
cheese. And the Russians advanced. She who had

refused to join the League of German Girls was
abducted by the SS and ordered to eat. And she ate
because you eat what you can during a war
when the guns are pointed at you.

She ate vegetable puddings as the skies
zigzagged with rockets. At night the guards
eased in to her room and had their way with her.
Margot Wolk. She ate eggs poached, scrambled,

over-easy. She cried with relief after surviving
a meal. Part of the Poison Brigade to save
a man who cried when dogs were shot in films.

Navajo Code Talkers, Iwo Jima

The code talkers
spoke in a language
learned centuries before
from lichen on spider rocks
In the language they learned
how day-to-night came to be
how light, air, water and earth
contain everything equally

No one knew what they were saying
but they knew the language
they were slapped for by nuns
when they spoke it in grammar school
These syllables were tangles of vines
and tall grass to the Japanese code breakers
The Navajos spoke as though
they were sowing seeds
of how to live
with Earth and Sky

Julius Rosenberg Murmurs from the Dead

Remember 1945. She didn't do it.
    She birthed our boys. She wanted to sing
on stage. She didn't do it. She didn't
    type it. And the it. You know the it.
Her sister-in-law did it. But Ethel
    didn't do it. Thought they'd charge her—
force me to finger co-conspirators
    which would save her.

Yes I was a communist. Yes I was a spy. I passed
    along inept sketches. At her trial she didn't cry,
not the weak woman the judge wanted her to be.
    You can shake a cloud like a blanket
let the mist spill out. And she didn't
    do it. No raindrops there. She didn't do it.
It took two extra jolts of the electric chair
    to kill her. She was that innocent.

Lyon Years Later

Still the clatter of jack boots in her head.
Simone sipping bone broth.
A soul as hard as oak, harder to get to.
Simone sipping bone broth.
Identical tears on her cheeks. Her sister
a resistance fighter, had her own nipples
pulled off with pliers. Simone's days
are wagers with silhouettes. Whose head

wasn't immersed in ammonia? What code
wasn't broken by shadows? If she were
only a cherry blossom, a solution
for a rodent problem, a tongue in a bell.
If the echo of jack boots didn't follow her.
If every black Citroen weren't Gestapo.
If the wind were only the wind
not the hum of a gun.

Survival

Her grandmother didn't survive Auschwitz
but Anna survived the preservatives
in Mrs. Butterworth's syrup, felt her own
inner flesh shielded from aging.
It made her snore longer and longer
every evening after eating half a dozen
flapjacks, soaking them in golden
decrescendos of the brown bottle
and the thick wedges of salted butter
that dripped over the chewy dough.

She remembered her mother's bread hands
kneading, and the tattooed number
on her mother's wrist shaking, saying *remember*
as if it could speak, remember the space
between happiness and angels. Live there.
Between Anna's blues and her harvest
of golden plums, she knows the hands
of mercy, and lives between the air's skin.

Napoleon's Penis

Yes it was severed
by his doctor during the autopsy.
Not an arm or a leg or the head.
And such a little penis that shrunk
to a piece of leather or
a shriveled little eel.

Impossible not to imagine Napoleon
shaking his tiny garden hose
with his left hand before battle
while his right hand warmed his war wound.
Years later, on display in Manhattan,
the penis shone under spotlights.
A maltreated strip of buckskin
said TIME magazine.

For a time the penis sat in a jar
under the bed of a urologist.
Imagine manipulating your own erection
while a strip of dried beef jerky
gathered dust beneath you.

Now bid at $100,000, the penis
is ready to bed corpses around the world,
ready to piss on Waterloo once more,
piss on the Russian winter.
In the end, it's all just
shake and dance.

Bob Beamon's Leap

Over riot police over the whole world watching
over the cheek-to-cheek dreams of Vietnamese soldiers
it was the leap of the century in Mexico City, 1968 Olympics,
spikes flying through sunlight, spread-eagled

over Khe Sanh and Tet over a Saigon general shooting
a suspect over Soviet hammers and sickles, tanks and troops,
planes assaulting Czechoslovakia. Bob Beamon
strode the runway, took off at an altitude of 7387 feet,

leaped over Kennedy and King's assassinations over the raised,
    black-glove
fists of John Carlos and Tommie Smith on the Olympic podium,
    hitch-kicked
over *Pueblo* sailors—prisoners flipping the bird at North Korea.
He flew over Nixon's nomination, Humphrey proud as punch,

leaped two feet farther in air thin as microfilm. He leaped over
Winfield Scott
marching through Mexico City, over jack 'o lanterns of October
over grieving sunflowers over complaints his leap was just a freak.
He leaped over jealous syllables at every altitude, feet extended

to prolong his flight under an afternoon chaste as cotton,
twenty-nine feet, two and a half inches. He flew farther than
    Apollo 8
circling the moon. He extended gravity in the long jump,
once the broad jump, now the broad horizon.

Haji Baba Lane

The sticky bus. The bus a Toyota truck.
Three benches. Twenty girls. The smell of dust.
The smell of face lightening cream. Scarves on heads.
Twenty girls. No windows. The plastic sheeting

>yellowed. A stamp of sky in the cracked corners.
>Three benches. Twenty girls. A bearded man
>in the road. *Stop the bus. Open the door.*
>The sun a scarlet orb floating in dust.

His peaked cap. The handkerchief over his nose
and mouth. *Who's Malala?* The bullets.
The pistol. Three benches. Twenty girls. *Who's
Malala?* No one speaks. They look at the girl.

>Three bullets. The bookish girl. The shots.
>The sound of rickshaws sputtering diesel in the street.
>What shoves away the bullets from her brain?
>It's the chemical equations chanted by girls in class.

It's the Urdu grammar memorized by girls.
It's girls drawing blood circulation diagrams
preparing to be doctors. Girls in school.
It's the girls. The girls. The girl.

Barlow Flats Camp, Big Sur, 1971

That night the Vietnam vets dropped acid
circled the fire and drew breaths
folded maple leaves onto their fingers
like gloves of blood.

They circled the fire and drew breaths
entered the forest nearly naked
flashed their gloves of blood.
Sunsets burned the horizon red.

They entered the forest nearly naked
smelled the minds of maples and pines
while sunsets burned the horizon red.
They smelled unexploded ordnance,

smelled the minds of lotus and bamboo
thousands of miles away.
They smelled unexploded ordnance
rickshaws and bodies they had shot

thousands of miles away the yellow
squash blossoms the plum moths
the rickshaws the bodies they had shot.
They searched dream zones for the dead.

The squash blossoms and plum moths
folded leaves onto their fingers.
They searched dream zones for the dead—
the Vietnam vets who dropped acid.

Coming Home

In the shadow of a pickup in Alabama
a man is pulling a comb
through greasy hair, tonguing a mint tic tac.
He has dreamed this house and gathered
warmth from afternoon sunshine.
The slow drum roll of leaf
against leaf jazzes up the slog
of autumn. These are the days of faith
and blunt voices, luck and fettuccini.
He edges up the sidewalk like a raj.
What he loves…what he loves—click—
the bloom of a bachelor button, the swirl
of wind through a chrysanthemum
is not what blooms and flows between
the rusty bicycle and tub of Drano:
no watery melodies through trees, only pop
cans scraping against his Iraq
War boots. He creases a footprint near
the door stoop. How long will the wild gusts
of desert sand reside within his wrist?
How many backfiring engines, bouts of desert flu
until he doesn't jump, thinking Molotov
Cocktails and roadside bombs will blow?
Instead of dreaming that he is hacking an ax,
he is knocking on the door, waiting for eternity,
waiting for the door to open, for the gin to fizz.

Eulogy for a Bullet

My brain might be the final resting place
for a bullet tooled from rubber, steel,

tin and tungsten. The cone tip
makes silent grooves through the air

when an unhappy student squeezes the trigger.
The bullet expands from my cerebrum

to cerebellum, lodges itself
beside the stored lines of verse in my brain

beside the lesson plans on Transcendentalism,
beside the memory of watching my daughter

walk across the room for the first time,
her young feet squishing the rug, her giggles

filling up the room, our clapping so loud
it sounded like gunshots.

Final Syllables

Mrs. Johannes Livingston cannot touch her stiff toes
unless she kneels the way she kneeled
scrubbed toilets and tiles
scrubbed bathtubs
scrubbed wooden floors
scrubbed baseboard heaters for wealthy women
scrubbed until the phantom noises of her MIA husband
disappeared
somewhere in the Mekong Delta
his bones in a ditch or a rice paddy or buried
in a shallow jungle grave
his dog-tags sluiced in muck and mud

Was or wasn't he MIA
What the Domino Theory
What the Gulf of Tonkin
Scrubbed and scrubbed What the
Somewhere the bullet that cracked his skull
or split his spleen
Somewhere covered in moss the bullet

    with his name on it
    with his blood on it
    with his sweat on it
What if she could scrub it shine it up
Would his face gleam in the copper sheen
Would she hear his final syllables
and remember the whispers
when they were married
when her knock-knees didn't ache
when the wind didn't slur
its consonants and vowels
and the language of winter wasn't punctuated
by rain

Of Wars

Never again Gina confirms
on Veterans Day
gripping her cigarette.
She text messages
her boyfriend
who will be her ex-boyfriend
in a matter of seconds.
Her thumb hovers
over the send button
same thumb she runs
over her tattoo.
Why does his kanji character
on her arm
always resemble
a half-eaten bear claw?
She is nearly numb
as a pie pan.
One button to push.
Just one to end
this war of all wars.

Don't Miss the Sale

One war is closing down like a furniture store
with 50% off corduroy sofas.
A new war on a new continent,
new enemies with laser guided weapons
leaps into action with new blasts,
new ways to puncture skin and break bones.
But no one trims lawns of the scattered old-dead.

The scattered new-dead wait for medics
to snap-chat their faces, post their memories
online. Enemies of the old-dead bundle up,
kiss and make up before they blast the next
blast, make more dead, resurrect mercy.
They shake night words like dice, spill them
on the billiard table, wait for the next sale.

Interrogation

Who races the black cloud?
    not the titanium leg of the veteran
    who leans on his crutch for a sundial
    and wanders the garden of sand

Who defends the dead?
    not flash floods or lizards
    or the sting of cactus tines
    not the purple heart

Who cares for the wounded hills?
    not salt not rain not the aim of a sniper
    or phosphorescence lost in the stars
    not the trigger finger

iii

Inspection

Are you wearing a wig?
    There's a point in the distance where the river
    meets itself. The river thinks ahead. The water
    streams through me, full-flush of guilt.
    There's a current in my breath as I inhale
    to say yes when Lamet beside me says no.
Son, are you leveling with me? the JG spits.
    No sir Lamet blushes. His wig, bushy-brown,
    flops on his neck. Adrenaline surges
    through me, itches my neck. Will my
    bobby pins fall out? Will my wig cap
    droop like Grandmother's stockings?
I've known for a long time you're wearing a wig.
    It's Lamet's first time wearing a short-hair wig.
    I've been wearing mine for months. My real hair
    falls to my shoulders, warms my ears.
    The JG can't remember my name
    since I don't wear a nametag.
Are you a wannabe girl, Lamet? Get a haircut.
    The JG's mustache wobbles before he speaks.
    We call him Miss Prissy. We know he wears
    sock garters to show his magnificent blue socks
    when he sits, crosses his legs. Never a shirt stain.
    Always a flick of red hair under his hat.
Where's your National Defense Medal?
    Standing still, I'm floating away from this whirlpool—
    a duck riding downstream bobbing around rocks
    and the whoosh of words that hiss like waterfalls.
    The JG steps into me. Expensive aftershave.
    He snorts and fingers my neck.

Boarding the MV from Monrovia

The Chief Mate tries to bribe me with bourbon
in coffee and a wide grin. There's a gap in that grin
a missing tooth. Maybe that's where he'll find

the Load Line certificate. He rummages through
papers, bottles, shackles—a bear poking his snout
in anthills, flicking bees from his paws,

about to rub up against a tree, scratch
his itches, roar that he's found the certificate.
The cabin smells of oil. A *Playboy* calendar

hangs on the bulkhead open to June. It's July
but Miss June smiles her bosomy smile. Tension
off-loads like a ferryboat. The bear bumbles,

grunts like a glacier calving, stomps, smashes
a basket before his thick paw produces
the certificate creased like starlight. His ragged breath

pants. *Where is the COFR?* I ask. He slaps down
the Dangerous Cargo Manifest, growls and grunts,
yanks a cabinet to test his strength. How soon

will fur rise from his hackles, his fangs
glint in weak light and the gnaw and gnashing
begin? Legend has it a woman becomes

a bear when her husband turns to sadness.
Has she become this man? If this were a painting,
anger would be tapping rhythm in a bear's eye,

his mind wrapped tight as ivy. I would be the echo
in the hollow corner with a heart of gray snow.
The bear would sharpen his talons on my bones.

Burial Detail

How many lies
have we told
to stay alive—
not enough
for the Coastie
we buried.
Death fears an AK-47.
Silence has forgotten
how to bluff music
back into a horn
playing Taps.
Happiness is caught
off guard. Some days
thunder talks dirty
to the angels.
We create answers
that erase themselves.
As much as we try
we can't trap a dream
mid-air.

The Midwatch

Self, remember the slender arm of the violinist
bowing across the strings, and the sound warm
as a chrysanthemum opening.
You are the flower, the strings, the arm

> not on guard duty, checking license plates
> checking ID. Trucks grind gears
> past the Main Gate. A siren howls
> like an urban hyena. A door slams.

Under the stagelights the hair on her arm
glistens like a silver meadow
while the cellist and flautist retrieve
the vowels and constellations of earth and sky.

> Philippe's drunk again, stumbles from the EM club,
> says it's flashbacks from the Mekong.
> I push him back to the barracks. He curses,
> spits, crunches gravel along the walkway.

Around and under you is silence
among the rhythms and plush cushions
of the concert hall, among the promises
made of sound, fingers like fire shadowing notes.

> A bell clanks-in customers across the street
> at the sub shop. Chunks of cheese line the window.
> The owner sucks on pickles, pounds down meatballs,
> slaps mayonnaise on foot-long sandwiches for a Coastie.

The moon is rising over the Gate, scaling the wall
like a commando, the air strangely cinnamon.
You are humming last night's melody and holding
her narrow elbow, ushering the night.

Philippe's getting married

    after getting divorced
already arguing
    with his next wife.
Traded women.
    Traded Army
for Coast Guard.
    Rack of medals
on his dress blues.
    Did a hitch in Nam.
Now in charge of armory.
    Locks it up.
Unlocks it. Likes to hold
    an M-16.
Likes to clean it.
    Swing it. Aim it.
Smirks at the JG.
    Smirks at the Chief.
How heavy is the hurt
    behind the smirk?
He snubs sleep, his eyes
    a Haitian voodoo.
He wanders where he wanders.
    Anyone else
and he'd have a Captain's Mast.
    The war stays with him.
A whispered echo
    rises in his voice,
a man in a cage
    of slant-light looking out
of venetian blinds.
    Is he the killer
or the killed in a film noir?
    If he smokes a Lucky,
the ash will linger
    like the stare of a cougar.

If he smirks in the steam heat,
    is there a knife,
am I the target, is my face
    a continent away
in a rice paddy, on a path in a village
    a gourd in my hands
a bomb in the gourd, a burst
    a blast, at last a flame
a flash of something
    to undo the smirk?

Freeway Back-up

I moo to the moo cows
gated in the truck beside me.
The walnut-size eye of one cow
looks into me, knows I'm
a meat-eater, knows I think
tenderloin, rack of ribs on the grill
and how I could use a thick pair
of cowhide gloves to clear
salmonberry thorns.
Ahead, a siren whines. Behind,
a horn hiccups, blares. The cow
moos. How smooth the skim milk
softened my granola this morning
a peach-on-my-cereal morning.
The song of a Swainson's thrush
snapped and hummed like Snagglepuss
and the blue blade
of an iris oozed like a negligee.
I'm not so bummed that I bounce
my horn because I'm late
for morning muster.

I bounce my horn as part of the music
that storms a morning
on the freeway. Kinda fun
like chewing cinnamon gum.
The cow nods at me and I nod back
not voyeurs of war
more like girls and boys
jumping on whoppie cushions
while the nailbiter growling in the Ford
behind us is sure she owns
the world, but her push buttons
don't function and she's grumped
herself into the hole of a geometry proof

she cannot solve. What if she mooed?
What if she gutted a sound
so loud she could outsprout
the weeds winding inside her
and heard joy carved in the air?

Between Taps And Reveille

I was tired but I didn't
                give in to Lamar
who said he could really
                dig making love
to me on the couch
                in Cynthia's house.
I wanted to be upstairs
                unbuttoning her blouse
in her room where the moon
                filled up her bedspread.
No I said No
                and said No a month later
between taps and reveille
                to Seaman Wilbur.
He climbed in my rack
                held my arm the way
we held M-16s, nuzzled
                them against our cheeks
hot in August sunshine
                aimed and fired.
Call it the summer
                of wrong loves
standing at attention,
                saluting, marching
past love, aiming,
                firing, missing,
reloading, claiming
                the hope, the better aim.

After Morning Muster

The Chief is filling his coffee cup,
joking, telling the one about the nun
drunk in the confessional booth. This week
she's swallowing vodka. Last week, Scotch.
Peterson, a seaman, is polite enough
to laugh, hoping he won't get
the midnight watch.

Beyond the cove the sea holds
our stories, whitecaps as high as the horizon.
A 44-footer hauls in the survivors
of a purse seiner. 5-foot, 10-foot,
20-foot waves. The sea gives its head
a wet-dog shake. Even when we are dry
we are in the water.

Jameson

Big hands. Badass. Slaps me so hard
    I fall down serving mashed potatoes
        on Thanksgiving dinner. He says,
Don't shake that spoon. I ain't no dog.
He isn't hiding from the draft
    but if he hadn't enlisted
        he'd be doing time for a crime
    Was it dealing? Was it stealing?
Was it break-and-entering? I don't ask.
    I don't look long at Jameson on-base
        or off-base. He's striking for Gunner's Mate.
    He snores on the lower bunk
two rooms over like a truck grinding gears
    going uphill, Grr. Grr.,
        but he can *yes sir, yes ma'am* off-base.
    We save lives, ma'am, his big hands
holding open a door for her
    then shoving me to the floor.

Dance of the Dungeness Crab

Before her new exoskeleton hardens,
she comes on to him in the eelgrass
and sandy bottom not by flirting

with her purple legs or her white-tipped claws
that clench oysters, tiny fish and clams.
She lets go her urine, so wonderfully

full of pheromones and he is on to her
tucking her in a pre-mating embrace.
Such summer love this holding,

this belly-to-belly nudge among the mussels
and barnacle reefs under the swell of waves
so coy in the silence of love

before she urinates on his antennae—
her greatest come-hither, her valentine-be-mine
in the low intertidal zone.

Above My Paygrade

Van Sickle yanks me off work detail
hands me a hard hat and we're off

to monitor a barge bunkering at ARCO,
but first he grinds the government van

up and around the smelter, over the bridge
to a tav. Ten AM. *Part of your training*

he winks and we kick a few chairs
up to the stage. Sandy's shaking her ass

around a pole. We hold longneck bottles of Bud.
Her tassels, gold as the stripes on the visor

of the commander back at base, whip the smoky air.
Van Sickle leans into me. *Are you cool with this?*

You are cool with this. You are, aren't you?
He slides a 5 spot under Sandy's G-string.

Part of the training. *Thanks Danny* she says.
His first name is Danny. Danny Van Sickle.

I'm learning names and what to monitor,
what to say, what not to say at 10 AM.

What Was That Book?

When I think of the woman I kissed
and lied to at the University of Virginia
pretending I was a freshman
on rush night, drinking in fraternities,
kissed her, hugged her
when I was in the Coast Guard,
on liberty, hitchhiking from base,

I think of her southern lips
that kept kissing, kept saying
I do not believe you,
I believe you,
I do not believe you
as she ran her fingers
over my crew cut that scraped
like sandpaper,

and I think of the sociology book
she carried and wonder if it taught her
the needs of a sailor
when he's not in uniform
when he thumbs the pages
when his enlistment stretches out
like an alphabet of dark clouds.

iv

Bowline

I am on the roof of my car knotting
    a bowline around a Christmas tree
        securing it to the rack.
            My daughter in the back seat licks a candycane
        while rain numbs my fingers.
    She is all rhythm, plugs a music
into her ears, kicks her legs.
    If I could wait until we were home, warm,
        dog not barking in the car and me not swearing
            like my father swore—but there's this knot:
    rabbit comes out of its hole,
runs around the tree, back into its hole.
I know this knot. My father taught me—
    and me thirteen, bat and glove in my hands,
        my friends throwing a ball in the street:
            Come on. Come on.
        His freckled, knobby fingers moved smoothly
    like hand puppets dancing, boring
to me then, alive to me now, the grace
    of a father in a gruff voice
        how to hold and tie up loose ends.

Returning Student

He was the little shit in class
who mouthed off until I
sent him into the hall,
jacked him against the wall

and inches from his face
told him never to say fuck, shit,
cock sucker or mother fucker
in my classroom. I tapped my finger

like a piledriver against his chest
told him not to show up stoned
ever again. *I'm not stoned* he blurbed.
Planets rotated in his eyes.

He was busted the next month for having sex
in the pool with an under-aged girl.

Damned if he didn't show up
two years later. Marine uniform.
Square-shouldered. Polite as yes sir.
He was off to Afghanistan, asked me

for advice. *You're a vet. What can you
teach me?* Thesis statements and proper
paragraphing hadn't worked.
You're the only one who told me like it is.

I wondered whose voice he was using.
Teach him? I nodded, returned his salute
and said, *Keep your ass down.*

The Teacher

A Nam vet with the 82nd Airborne,
he told stories of trench toe,
jungle rot, malaria, was examined
annually for Agent Orange,

taught a class on Nam
to high school seniors
only he didn't go and there was no
trench toe, no Incoming,

no malaria and his hip didn't hurt
from humping through the jungle.
The American Legion routed him out,
exposed him like an open wound.

So he was a poser, was shamed,
a scum, a liar and he resigned
ran out of town, sold his house,
the favorite teacher in school.

And still we want to hold him
like a brother in battle, a colleague,
feed him, ask him what war
is raging through him,

what unfinished fight is he fighting
what PTSD nightmares
pass through him like ghosts
and have filled him with terror since birth.

Sea and Sky Followed Him from Berth to Berth

When he came back home
he moved into an urn

earlier than he might have
earlier than ashes

only flashes of a fallen idol.
He moved but didn't move

and only knew himself
by the smell of the sea.

Two dogs—himself and his other self—
chased each other's tails

became one tail. They said they
never should have met.

They said it and they meant it
and they blinked at the shadow

of his frame that sat still
on the floor gulping air.

Navigating My Persona

I stood stunned when the pimp
    tried to set up my fifteen-year-old self with a hooker.
    Why do I remember I leaned against a jewelry store
        and a diamond ring gleamed in the window?
    I caught a city bus home. My hazy head mumbled
    something like music which was indistinguishable
from the backfiring of a diesel truck. My head pounded
    like a stallion demanding hay.
        What of flesh, what of love. The pimp's trousers
            were as baggy as an altar boy's gown.
        He might as well have
put his hands down my pants. My soul rolled
between the quills of a porcupine and the howls
    of a crime scene. It did its thing.
        The insomnias of October
relaxed into a percussion of leaves. These days
        the twenty-seven bones in my lover's hands
    spend all night partying on my front side/back side,
My soul finds an exit wound, wanders back to the curb.
    I shudder. The pimp speaks in a coach's voice,
        urges me on like it's fourth and goal.

Smoke Edges

Last night my dreams were full
of the assistant attorney general's boys
high school boys he taught

about law, tall spider of a man
who stayed past midnight in their minds.
How seamless his grace slipped into them.

Thin smile, thin as minced garlic,
smooth as their mother's lace. How he
helped them rustle with their coats.

How a boy's hand bumped his arm
and the general placed it back but not
where it should be. How he invited them

to his house. A weekend of boys.
How the whole house smelled of cloves.
Palms of boys. Mouths.

Last night the cries of one boy now a man
smoking, secrets unperishable. The ivy
on the deck wove into his thinking.

The general's dead bones dropped
their weight on him and the backyard
stream lengthened its shadow.

Infinity

Infinity winds its way over snowgrass and seedpods,
bladed winds of the prairie, down and around an arroyo,
up and over sandspits, sits like a Buddha
breathing in the world through its senses.

Infinity rubs itself raw between the empty spaces of sky.
For fun during high rains, it tries to drown itself,
knowing it cannot die. It is a superhero. It is Infinity,
biding its time in back eddies inhaling a river,
finning around rocks older than the earth's core.

When you're infinity, why not go on seeing
with the golden eye of a spider
crawling over bones and desert scrub brush
looking to the horizon, always the horizon
when a horn-rimmed owl arcs over the clouds.

Infinity would like to bed down under the sweet scent
of a hemlock tree, know the noise of a dragonfly sleeping,
wake to sunlight among the lost shadows
of the moon it has used for a pillow. It imagines itself
lemon-yellow as skunk cabbage, lighting up a swamp.

Some days infinity wants to sleep for infinity
but it needs earth, air, water, fire, needs to lean
like a lily into the sun, follow the shallow sky
feel the ground breezes massaging like fingers
unknotting piriformis muscles.

Infinity needs to stretch, curl itself into a ball,
meditate like a frog, lie down naked in dew grass,
roll over until the cold and sweet clover have
rinsed it clean, refreshed it pure as a willow herb.

While currents walk on water and bees go on buzzing,
infinity becomes its own divinity in its own body,
goes on long after we are gone and our words
find their own language to bless themselves
in the voice of an iris.

Lifelong

That year I drove back and forth
from my parents' house to my house

from changing my father's diapers
to toilet training my daughter.

It was the year of the bathroom
snapping on underpants/diapers

or celebrating pee-pee victories
my daughter no longer afraid she would fall in

be flushed down the toilet as she
had watched her golden pee be flushed away.

It was the year of poop and pee or shit and piss,
how we become human or lose our humanity,

the angry dementia mind, frantic
when it can't control its fluids

or the ecstatic, popsicle-victory joy
of peeing perfectly on a porcelain throne.

I shifted gears across the island feeling
throned and de-throned; ahead the years

of ghost stories and watching a ghost slip past me,
the road winding through pines and leather ferns.

The Dead Are Still Shaving

They break into boarded-up houses
looking for razors. They cannot see themselves
in the failed mirrors. The fine line
between their upper lips and noses has become
jumbled like a ball of silver yarn. The dead

pull on grubby jeans and boots, pour stale coffee
still on the stove. The caffeine has no kick.
On the porch they light cigarettes
but do not have the breath to inhale
exhale the first sins of morning.

They write *peach ice cream* on a shopping list.
The letters disappear like the flavor. The dead sit down
on couches ready to argue curfew time
with their daughters, and who will use
the car, who will vacuum the back room,

who will mow, weed, prune. But no daughter is arguing.
No daughter is licking fruity lip gloss from her lips.
The dead miss the way their shadows
enter a room before they do and soften the light.
They climb on exercise bikes and pedal.

After half an hour there is no sweat.
The heart monitor reads 00 and still they pedal
faster, going nowhere. Outside, they wander off
ready to discard the afterlife the way a hang glider
discards one valley for another.

For the Last Time

A father in fatigues is drinking coffee
for the last time folding his napkin,
handing in his tray, knotting his boots,
belching in the barracks

saying *pardon me* for the last time,
slightly blushing the way he blushes
when he hears his wife whisper
their whisper at home.
He stands at attention
wonders for the last time if the shine
on his boots will pass inspection.

In the blue-black sky outside,
dawn drifts like an unhitched dinghy.
His hair will keep growing,
toenails keep growing for
the last time. But this time
he boards a truck, jumps off,
steps into the trees, bends,

touches the dust above an IED
the way he touched his daughter
for the first time, minutes after
she was born, her skin soft as water.

Before Draft Numbers

Remember those constellations like push pins
on a wall map? We stretched invisible
string from pin to pin, pretended we
visited them in spaceships. Remember

sleeping bags covered in dew, rock 'n' roll
on the transistor radio? We broke out
in hives and goosebumps: boys
in a pasture fighting hay fever,

drinking Hire's Root Beer, munching nuts
and potato chips; we were rock stars.
One of us jumped up, fist to his mouth
microphone to the universe, belted out

a sound he thought was music. For a moment
the frogs stopped croaking. The Big Dipper
bore down its stagelights. The singer
stuttered a jitterbug dance, pranced

around tall grass and thistles. We tackled him,
tickled him, rolled him over. He laughed
so loud it ran up and down his body
like a berserk hamster chasing carrots.

Finger Waltz with Jazz

A fold of fingers
smoothing skin
easing rhythms of drums
piano and guitars
what a dance of lips
does what a cloud does
cooling heat from a stone

Inside us the hum
of a long song
a loose weave of wind
that warmed us
held us all evening
the way ribs of the earth
hold a heart

About John Davis

John Davis is the author of two poetry collections, *Gigs* and *The Reservist*, and a veteran of the United States Coast Guard. His work appears in several journals including *DMQ Review, Iron Horse Literary Review,* and *Poetry Northwest.* After teaching high school for forty years, he now lives with his partner on an island in the Salish Sea and moonlights in blues and rock 'n' roll bands.

Also by John Davis

Gigs
Blues in D minor, big bellies over factory belts, and Elvis Presley license plates—*Gigs* is a collection of poems that shows us the gentle beauty of ordinary life. Davis's language breathes, without labor. His metaphors fit tight. And the rhythm of each word keeps pace with our innermost beats. Absolutely every poem in this book hammers a rightly strung chord.

To learn more about
Flat Sole Studio
and our other projects,
visit us at *flatsolestudio.com*
or scan the QR code below.

www.ingramcontent.com/pod-product-compliance
Lightning Source LLC
LaVergne TN
LVHW041713060526
838201LV00043B/714